Tatsuki Fujimoto

I love *The Texas Chainsaw Massacre!*

Tatsuki Fujimoto won Honorable Mention in the November 2013 Shueisha Crown Newcomers' Awards for his debut one-shot story *Love Is Blind*. His first series, *Fire Punch*, ran for eight volumes. *Chainsaw Man* began serialization in 2018 in *Weekly Shonen Jump*.

2

SHONEN JUMP Manga Edition

Story & Art **TATSUKI FUJIMOTO**

Translation/AMANDA HALEY
Touch-Up Art & Lettering/SABRINA HEEP
Design/JULIAN [JR] ROBINSON
Editor/ALEXIS KIRSCH

First published in Japan in 2018 by SHUEISHA Inc., Tokyo.
English translation rights arranged by SHUEISHA Inc.

Printed in the U.S.A.

Published by VIZ Media, LLC
P.O. Box 77010
San Francisco, CA 94107

10
First printing, December 2020
Tenth printing, April 2022

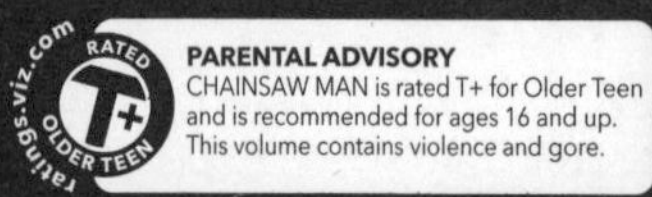

CHAINSAW MAN

2

CHAINSAW vs. BAT

Tatsuki Fujimoto

CHARACTERS

Denji

A young man-slash-Chainsaw Devil who carries his partner Pochita inside him. He's always true to his desires. Likes Makima, the first person to ever treat him like a human being.

Pochita

Chainsaw Devil. Gave up his heart to Denji, becoming part of his body.

Makima

The mysterious woman in charge of Public Safety Devil Extermination Special Division 4. Can smell Devil scents.

Aki Hayakawa

Makima's loyal subordinate. Denji's senior at Public Safety by three years, he's assigned to keep an eye on him.

Bat Devil

Was hiding after being injured by humans. Uses dirty tricks like taking hostages.

Power

Blood Devil Fiend. Egotistical and prone to going out of control. Her cat Meowy is her only friend.

STORY

Denji is a young man who hunts Devils with his pet Devil-dog Pochita. To pay off his debts, Denji is forced to live in extreme poverty and worked like a dog, only to be betrayed and killed on the job without ever getting to live a decent life. But Pochita, at the cost of the pooch's own life, brings Denji back—as Chainsaw Man! After Denji buzzes through all their attackers, he's taken in by the mysterious Makima, and begins a new life as a Public Safety Devil Hunter.

At Public Safety HQ, Denji is assigned to the squad of Makima's subordinate Hayakawa, but they clash from day one. While Hayakawa has a strong conviction to kill Devils, Denji, who never had anything but simple dreams, has only just discovered a new life goal—to touch some boobs. As Denji deliberates how to achieve his dream, he's paired up with a buddy—the Blood Devil Fiend Power. Denji is none too happy to be jerked around by this arrogant new partner. When Power offers to let him touch her chest if he saves her pet cat Meowy from another Devil, though, he jumps right on board! The duo heads straight for the spot where the Bat Devil awaits, but it's a trap, and Power was in on it. Once the Bat Devil regenerates by drinking Denji's blood, he eats not only Meowy, but Power too. Relating to Power's sadness over losing her precious pet, Denji faces off against the Bat Devil!

CONTENTS

Chapter 8: Chainsaw vs. Bat

ARRGH ?!
RAAH!!
ZASH

本自動車商会
KRA
SH

OW, OW, OW...
UHN... GNNGH ...

AH... AH...

IDIOT!
YOU'RE GONNA GET EATEN!

bump
YEEK!

tmp tmp tmp

YOU LET A HUMAN GET AWAY ...?!
BUT YOU'RE A DEVIL! WHAT IS IT YOU WANT...?!

TO SPLIT YOUR BELLY OPEN!
AND TOUCH THOSE BOOBS!

THOOM
DUH!!

GROHHH!
BRK
SH
TAM
CAN A FOOL WHO PROTECTS HUMANS...
grk

AHHH... AH!
AHH...
...CUT THROUGH THIS?!
HWO
OO

WHOA!
Umf!

MY CHAINSAWS CAN RETRACT?!

SUCH STRENGTH IN THAT PUNY BODY!

WHY WOULD YOU USE THAT STRENGTH TO SAVE HUMANS?!

SHWOOO
...Stupid Life!!
BAM
GYAH !!

OHH...
NYOOP
HO HA HA HA HA AH HA!!
PO PA PA PA PA PA PO!!
PAAH!!
GH

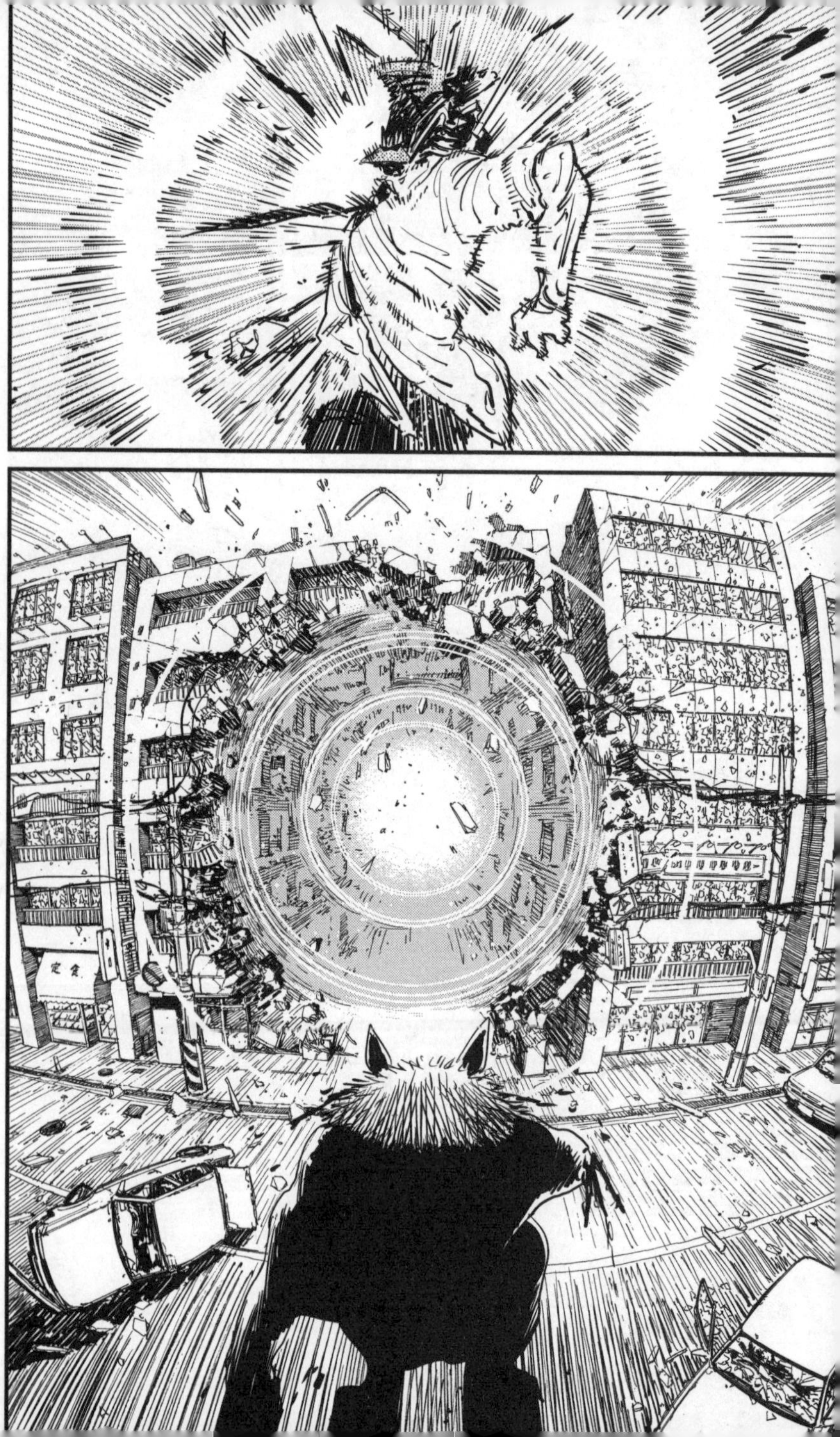

定食

AH?!

NGH... UUGH...

BDR
OOOM

FIRST, I MUST REGEN-ERATE!
THIS BLOOD REEKS OF TOBACCO, BUT I'LL TOLERATE IT RIGHT NOW...

WHOOM
HOW... ARE YOU ALIVE...?
CUZ EVEN THOUGH I'VE BEEN NOTHIN' BUT PATIENT...
...THROUGH A WHOLE BUNCH OF AWFUL CRAP...

...I STILL HAVEN'T TOUCHED 'EM EVEN A LITTLE!!
EEEEEEEEEEEE
VRRRR
ST—
Oof!
WHMP
STAY AWAY FROM MEEE!!

WH
AMM
GAH ?!

GARAARGH!
VRBEEEE

Chain
saw
man

Chapter 9: Rescue

BRING ME A HUMAN IF YOU WANT THE CAT TO LIVE.
ALL LIVES ARE EQUALLY TRIVIAL.
IT'S MERELY A CAT.
DASH

WHAT A FOOLISH REASON.

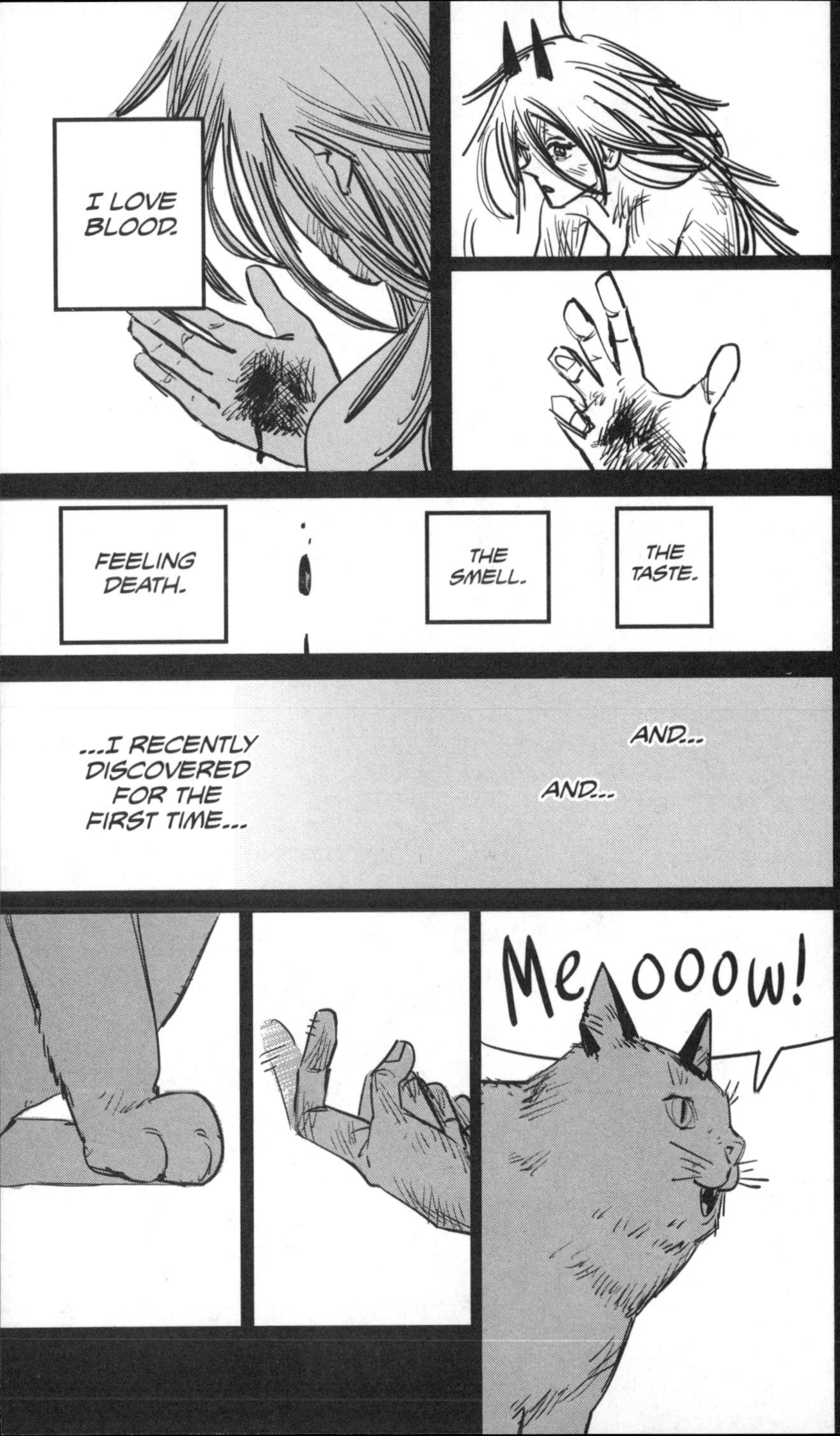

I LOVE BLOOD.

THE TASTE.

THE SMELL.

FEELING DEATH.

AND...

AND...

...I RECENTLY DISCOVERED FOR THE FIRST TIME...

Meooow!

THAT BLOOD IS NICE...
...AND WARM...

Meooow.

WHY DID YOU SAVE ME...?

I TRIED TO KILL YOU...

Meeew!

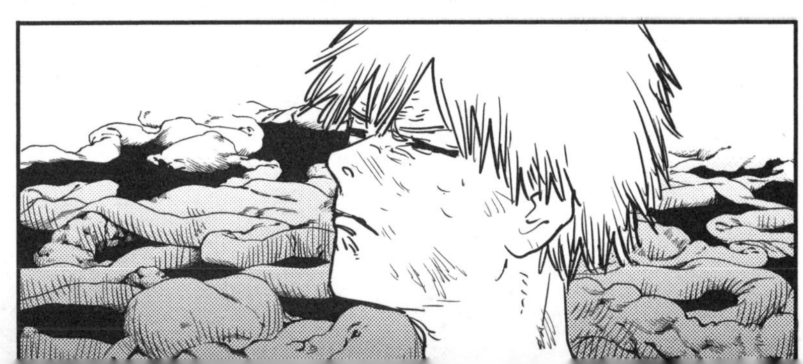

squeeze
squeeze
WHAT A FOOLISH REASON...

I'M SORRY I DECEIVED YOU.

MEOWY SUR-VIVED.
I'LL LET YOU TOUCH MY CHEST.

Awww yeeaaah!!
Ah!

Aaaaah?!
Owwww!!
AWW!
THE...
...PAIN...

CHO
MP

CAN YOU MOVE...?

NOT A FINGER ...

TAKE MEOWY AND RUN!

BDROOM

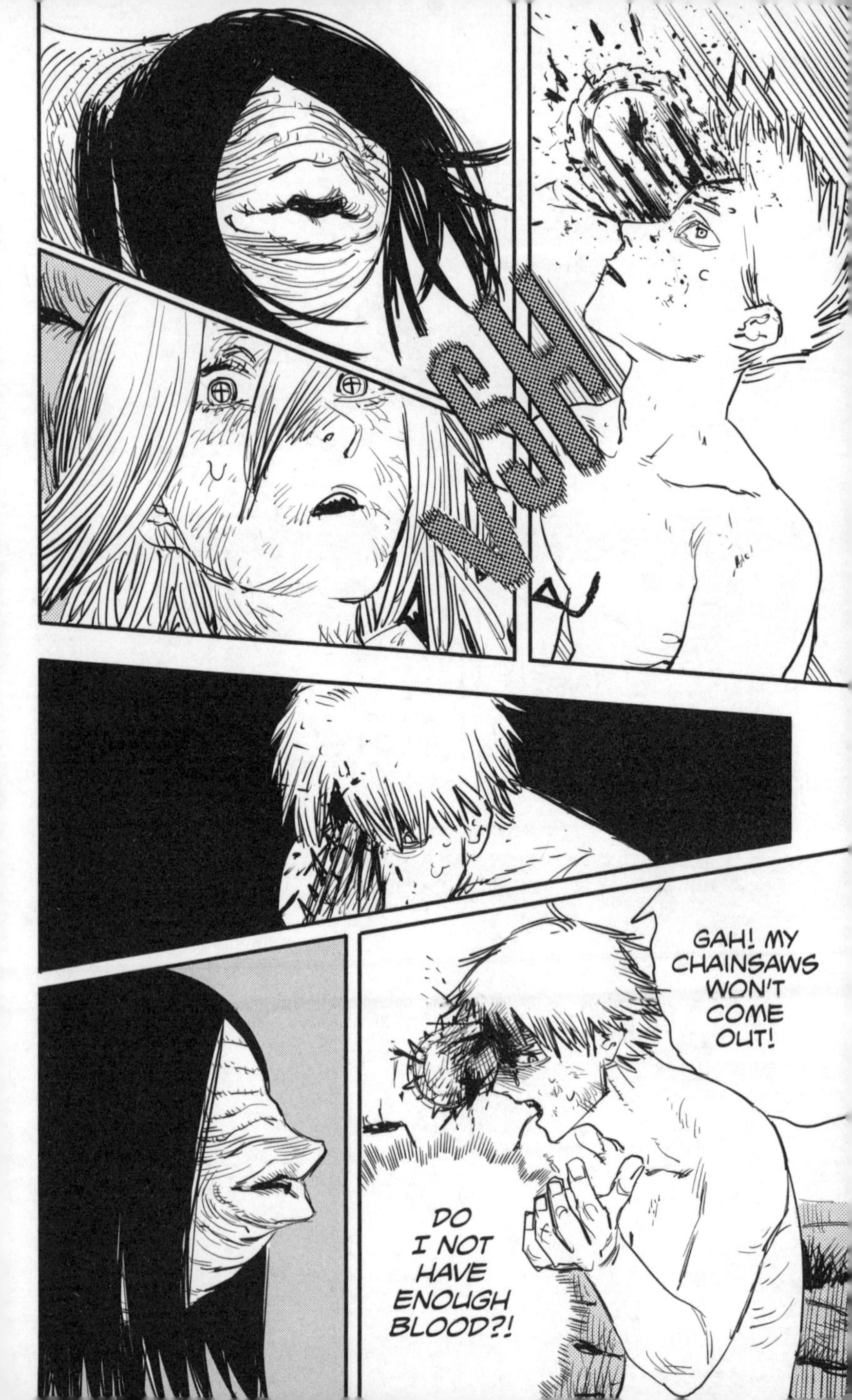
SCH
GAH! MY CHAINSAWS WON'T COME OUT!
DO I NOT HAVE ENOUGH BLOOD?!

Cafe
LIKE, JUST WHEN I FIIINALLY FOUND HIIIM...
YOU'RE THE ONE WHO KILLED BATTY, AREN'T YOUUU?
HE WAS MY BOY-FRIEND!

OOH... ON CLOSER INSPECTION, YOU HAVE A CUTE FACE...

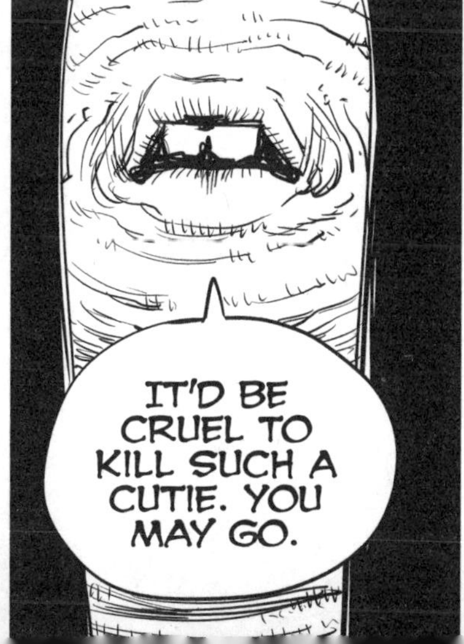
IT'D BE CRUEL TO KILL SUCH A CUTIE. YOU MAY GO.

AND THOSE TWO BEHIND ME...?
I'LL KILL THEM.

oo!
Pt

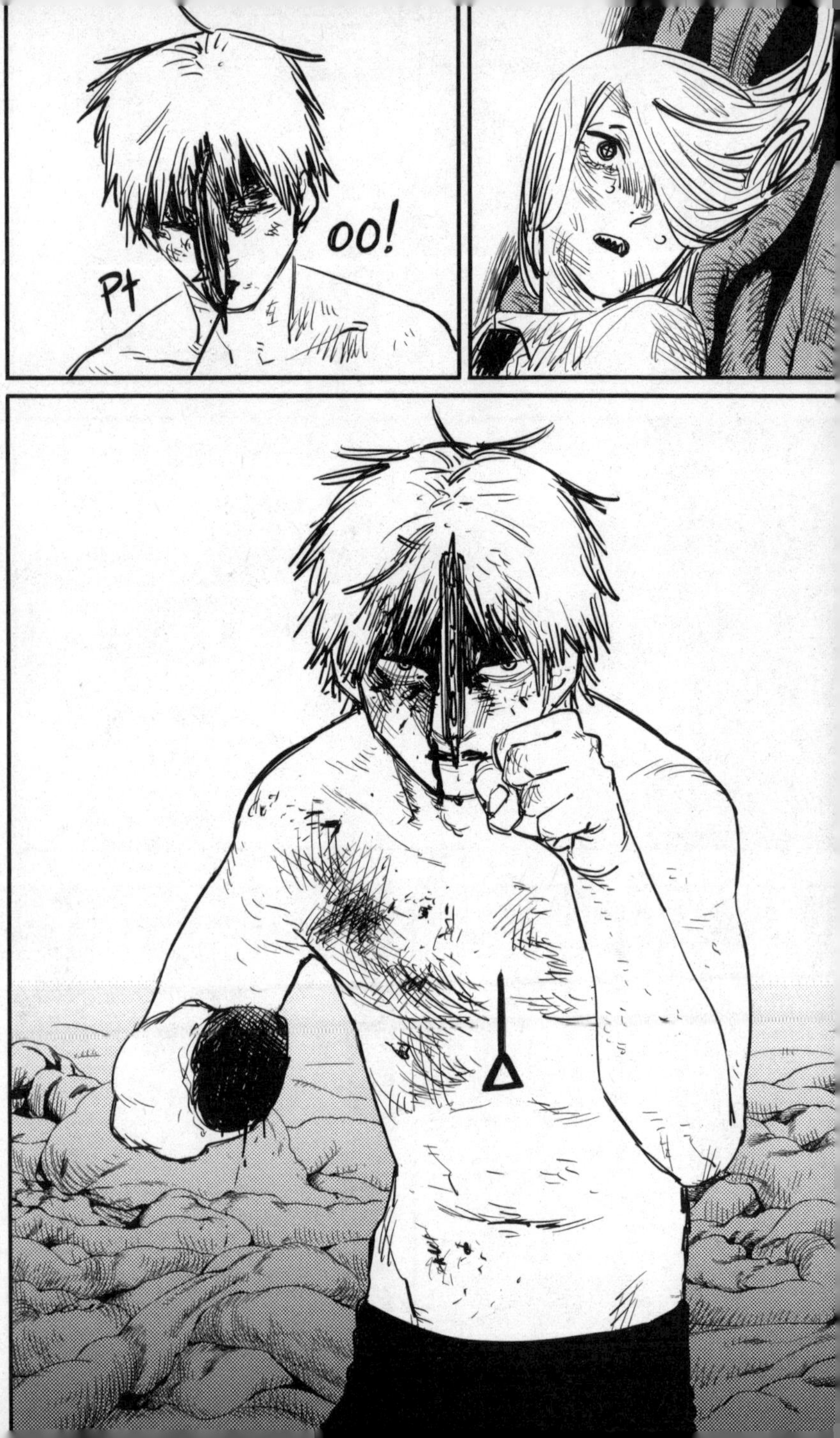

THEN DIE!

Chain
saw
man

Chapter 10: Kon
WOULD HE REALLY FIGHT A DEVIL LIKE THIS...
...MERELY TO TOUCH SOME BREASTS...?

UGH!!
YOU'RE KIDDING ME, RIGHT ...?!

BAT AND I DREAMED OF EATING ALL THE HUMANS TOGETHER...
AN IMPOSSIBLE DREAM, BUT SUBLIME AND BEAUTIFUL...
BAT GOT KILLED BY THIS PATHETIC LITTLE PUPPY DOG?!

AND IT'S BEEN SHATTERED BY SOME INSIGNIFI-CANT PUPPY DOG.
IT'S A SHAME ABOUT THAT CUTE FACE, BUT YOU NEED TO DIE.

sh
fw

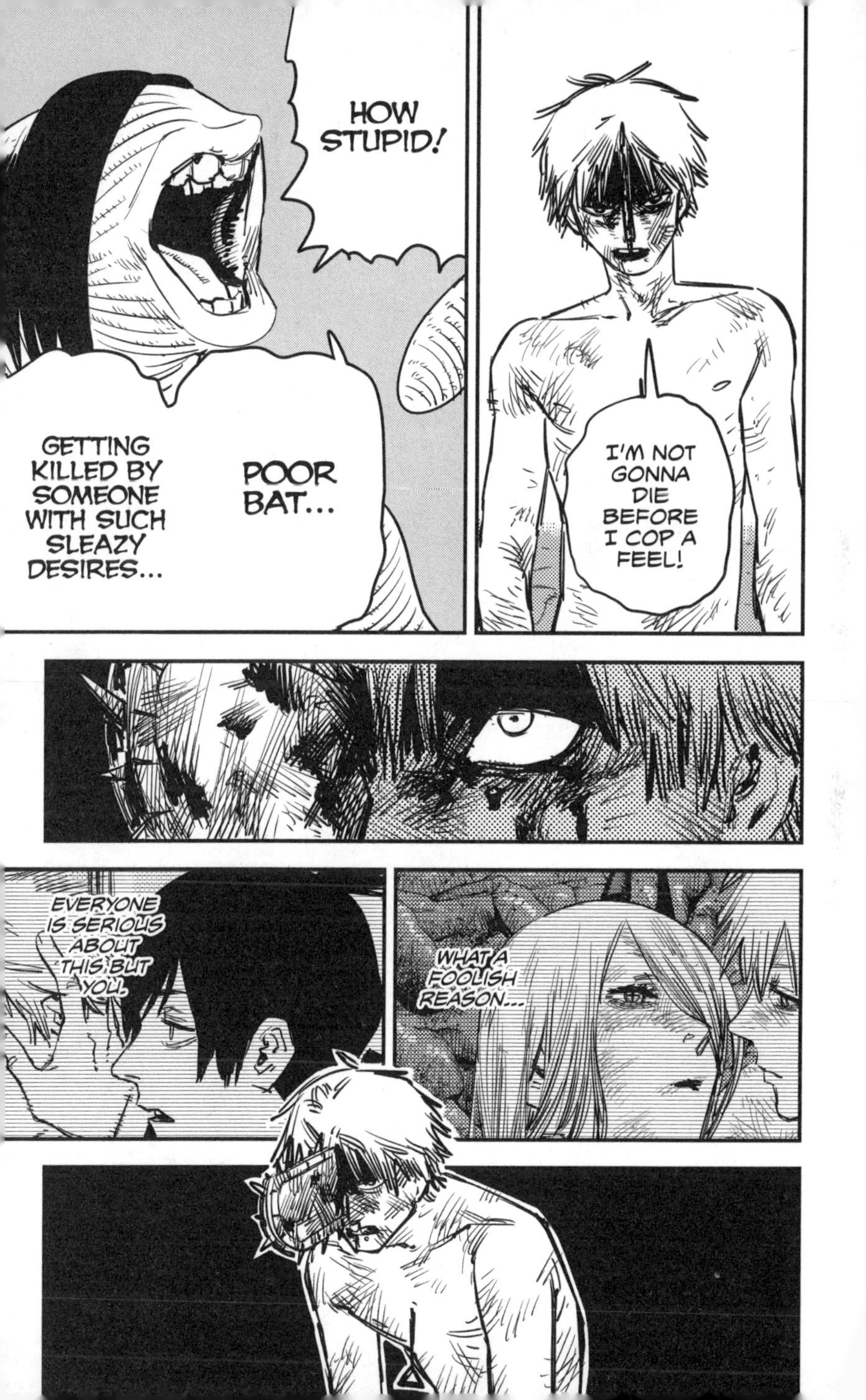

WHAT A FOOLISH REASON...

EVERYONE IS SERIOUS ABOUT THIS BUT YOU.

OHHH...

AH...

...RAH!!

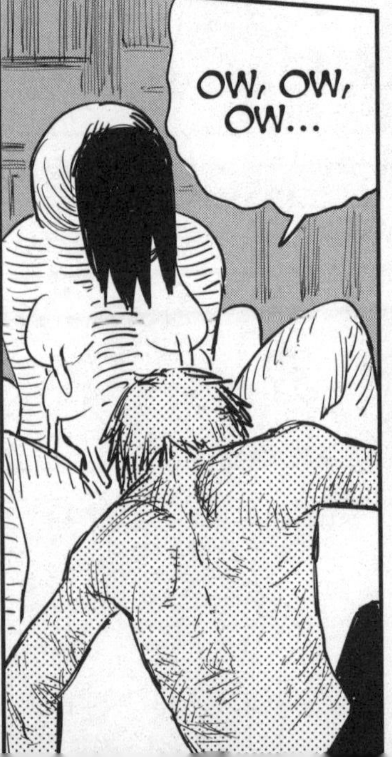

YOU AAAALL GOTTA LOOK DOWN ON THE STUFF I DO...
REVENGE?
PROTECT-ING YOUR FAMILIES?
SAVING A CAT?
BLAH, BLAH, BLAH!
YOU GUYS ALL GOT BIG IMPORTANT DREAMS? LUCKY YOU!!
LET'S HAVE A DREAM BATTLE THEN! YEAH, A DREAM BATTLE!!

IF I RIP YOU APART...
AW, HE'S BARKING! HOW DARLING!
HE YAPS AS MUCH AS A PUPPY!
...THEN THAT MAKES YOUR DREAM WORTH LESS THAN TOUCHING BOOBS!!
ALL RIGHT! I'LL EAT YOU UP!!
GA HA HA!! GO AHEAD!!
IF YOU CAN BEAT ME IN A DREAM BATTLE, THAT IS!!

HE'S A DEMON ...

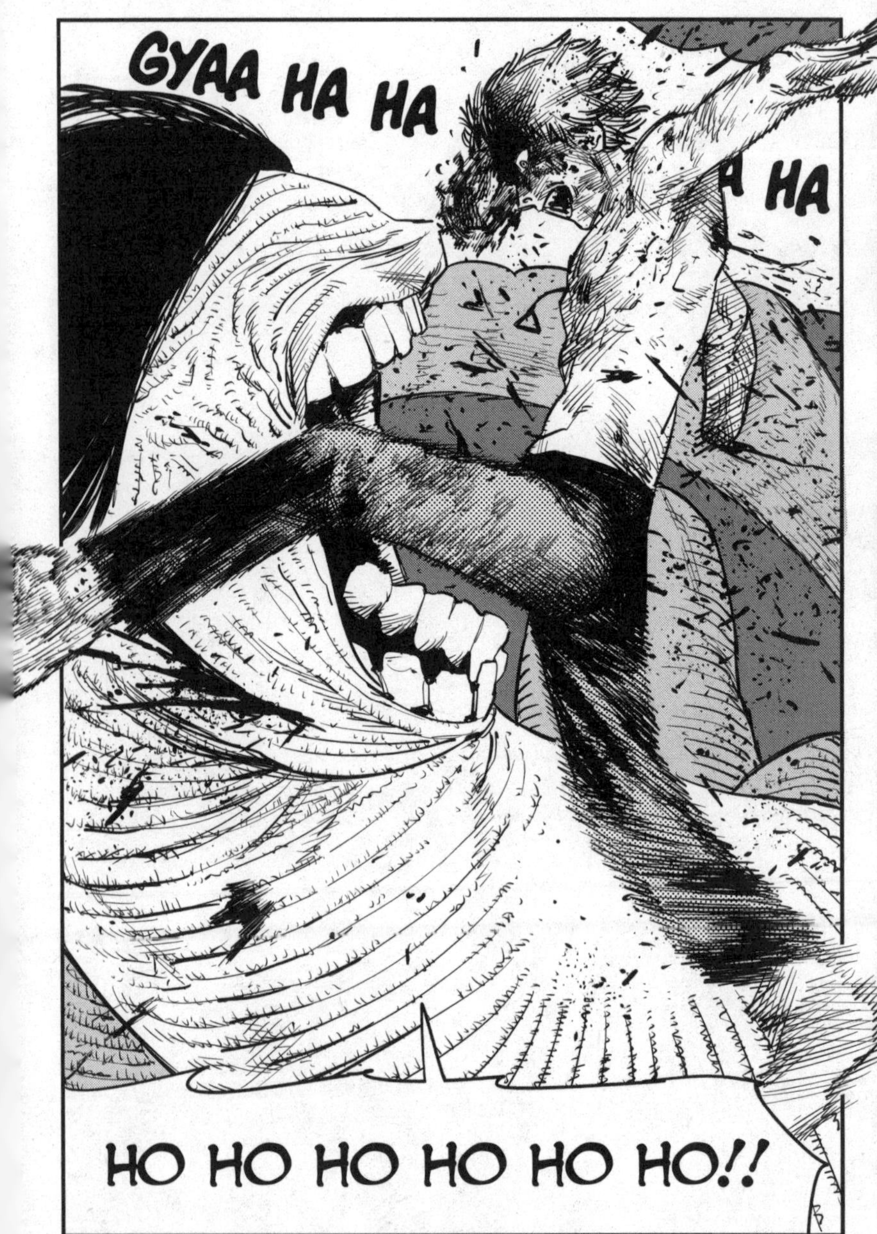
GYAA HA HA
A HA
HO HO HO HO HO HO HO!!

SHHHM
P

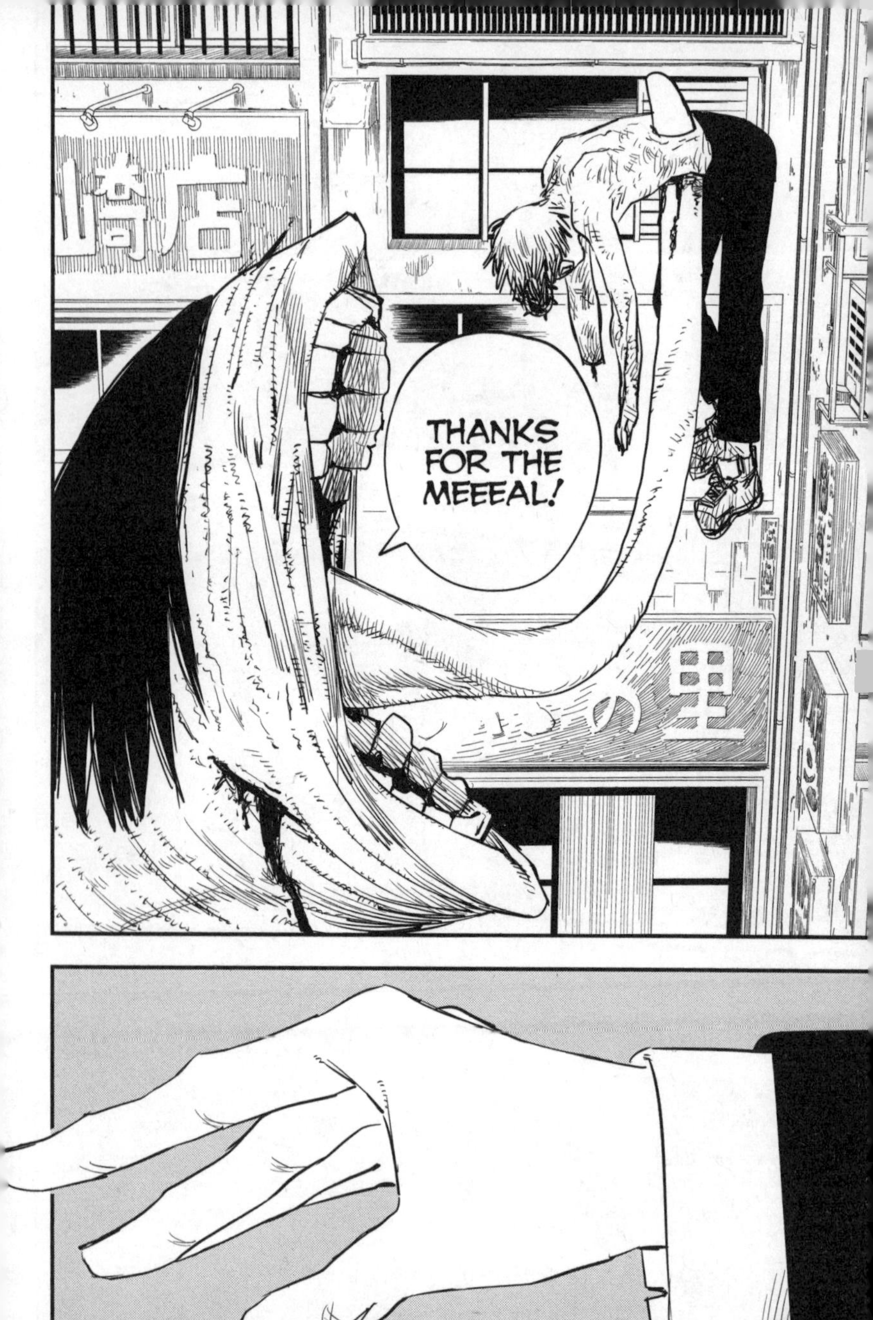
THANKS FOR THE MEEEAL!
崎店
の里

ョップ
特報

KON.

CHOMP

AH... HUH ...?

THIS'S THE *LEECH DEVIL.*

CAN I SWALLOW IT?

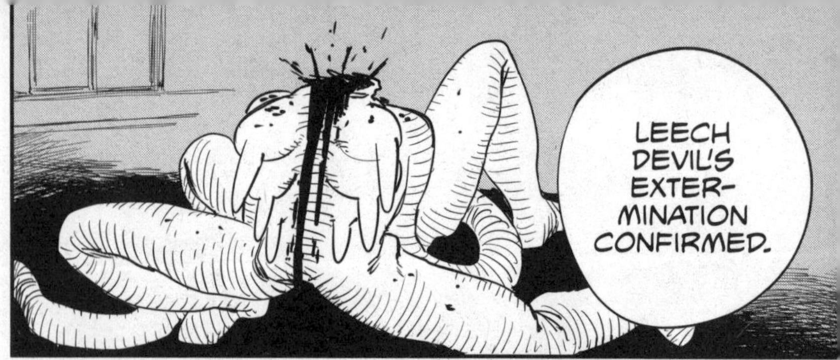
LEECH DEVIL'S EXTER-MINATION CONFIRMED.

NEWBIES, AID AND EVACUATE THE SURVIVORS!
YES, SIR!
Y-YES, SIR!

HIMENO, AS OUR SENIOR, YOU KEEP WATCH FOR DEVILS, PLEASE!
YOU GOT IT.

THE DREAM BATTLE ... I...
I... THE DREAM BATTLE...

ARRRRGH!!
YOU AND THE BLOOD FIEND ARE TO BE DEBRIEFED!

WHAT ABOUT MEOWY ...?!

Meowww!

THE CAT WILL GO TO A VETERINARY HOSPITAL FOR A FULL CHECKUP!

Chainsaw man

Chapter 11: Compromise

I GUESS IT REATTACHED ITSELF WHEN YOU GOT A BLOOD TRANSFUSION.
YOU REALLY ARE LIKE A DEVIL.

HEY, YOU WERE TALKIN' ALL CHUMMY TO A DEVIL YOURSELF!
I SAW IT, MAN.

YOU REALLY DON'T KNOW A THING, DO YOU?

DEVIL HUNTERS MAKE CONTRACTS WITH DEVILS. THAT'S HOW WE FIGHT.

I'M IN A CONTRACT WITH THE ***FOX DEVIL.***

IN EXCHANGE FOR BORROWING THE FOX'S POWER, I FEED IT PART OF MY BODY. THAT'S THE DEAL.

THIS TIME, I FED IT SOME SKIN.

POWER'S A GOOD ONE, Y'KNOW.

DEVILS DESIRE THE DEATHS OF HUMANS. ALWAYS.
FIENDS ARE THE SAME.

SECURITY CAMERA FOOTAGE CONFIRMS THAT THE TWO OF YOU LEFT YOUR PATROL AREA.

ALSO, THERE WAS A LARGE AMOUNT OF YOUR BLOOD IN THE BUILDING WE BELIEVE THE BAT DEVIL WAS HIDING IN.

YOU ALMOST GOT KILLED BY THE BLOOD FIEND, RIGHT?

WEIRD... WONDER WHAT'S UP WITH THAT...

I DON'T KNOW WHY, BUT YOU'RE SYMPATHIZING WITH A DEVIL AGAIN.

IT SEEMS SOMEONE NAMED DENJI GAVE HER HIS JACKET, SO WE CAME BY TO RETURN IT.
THANK YOU SO MUCH FOR SAVING MY LITTLE GIRL RECENTLY...

I SAW HE WAS WEARING THE PUBLIC SAFETY UNIFORM... SO I WANTED TO SAY THANKS...
A DEVIL CRASHED INTO MY WORKPLACE, AND THIS GUY WARNED ME I'D GET EATEN, SO I RAN...

IT WAS THIS DEVIL WITH A *CHAINSAW* LODGED IN ITS HEAD, AND...
IT SAID, "I DON'T CARE ABOUT SOME MAN'S STUPID LIFE!" AND THEN THAT DEVIL THREW MY CAR, *WITH ME IN IT!*

BUT THERE WERE NO CASUALTIES THIS TIME.
SO IF YOU'LL ACCEPT JUST ONE CONDITION, I'M WILLING TO OVERLOOK THIS INCIDENT.

IF I INVESTIGATE FURTHER AND REPORT THIS TO THE HIGHER-UPS, BOTH THE BLOOD FIEND YOU COVERED FOR...
...AND YOU WILL BE PUT DOWN.

shff

WHEN I TELL YOU TO DO SOMETHING, YOU DO IT.

YOU'RE A DUMB BRAT WITH NO MORALS.
I'VE BEEN DOING THIS FOR LONGER THAN YOU, AND I'D LIKE TO THINK I STAND FOR SOCIAL JUSTICE.

HOW'S THAT SOUND?
ANSWER ME IF YOU UNDER-STAND.

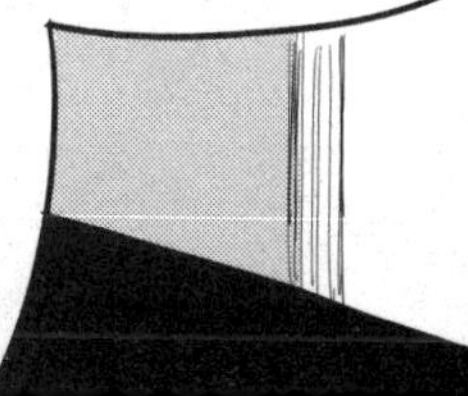
IF YOU JUST DO AS I SAY, YOU CAN PROTECT THE STANDARD OF LIVING YOU HAVE NOW.

sniff
sniff

I'M GONNA TAKE STUFF JUST AS SERIOUSLY AS YOU.

SO YOU CAN COUNT ON ME BIG-TIME.

FOR NOW, LEARN TO SPEAK WITH SOME RESPECT.

SURE. I'LL CONSIDER THAT FOR YA TOO.

k/ak

SEE? I TOLD YOU I WAS INNOCENT!
NOW THAT YOU KNOW IT, GET THESE THINGS OFF OF ME!
YOU SURE ABOUT THIS?
IF LITTLE MISS FIEND HERE KILLS SOMEBODY ONE DAY, IT'LL BE ON YOU FOR LOOKING THE OTHER WAY, AKI.

clik
WE ARE DEVIL HUNTERS.
WE OUGHT TO USE EVERY TOOL AT OUR DISPOSAL TO DO OUR JOB— EVEN DEVILS AND FIENDS.
BUT ENEMIES ARE ENEMIES... WE'RE *ONLY* USING THEM.
I HAVE NO INTENTION OF ***GETTING FRIENDLY*** WITH ONE.

HEY, HEY, HEY!
WHAT A CRAMPED HOME YOU HAVE!

I WANT YOU TO LEND ONE OF YOUR ROOMS TO POWER.

I THINK YOU COULD BE A GOOD LEASH FOR DENJI AND POWER.
Waaah!

WHY ARE YOU PUTTING ALL THE DANGEROUS ONES AT MY PLACE?

BECAUSE I TRUST YOU MORE THAN ANYONE.

OH... YES, MISS.

PLUS, IT WOULD BE WEIRD TO HAVE HER LIVE HERE INDEFINITELY.
YEAH...
DON'T WORRY. POWER SAID SHE COULD BE GOOD. IT'LL BE FINE.
I SEE.

I *HATE* VEGETABLES! BEGONE!
WHAT ?!
CARROT!
DON'T THROW VEGETA- BLES!
HEY!! DON'T YOU KNOW THAT'S DISRESPECTFUL TO THE FARMERS WHO GREW THOSE VEGGIES?!
YOU DEVIL!

YOU STINK!!
TAKE A BATH!
I'M THE TYPE WHO SELDOM BATHES!

IT STINKS!!

FLUSH IT!

THE TOILET?
I'M THE TYPE WHO SELDOM FLUSHES TURDS!

WHAT'S THE BIG DEAL...?
YOU HUMANS ARE SO SENSITIVE!
AREN'T THEY, MEOWY?

HEY, YOU.
AH!

SCRUB
SCRUB

WHAT, DEVILS CAN'T EVEN FLUSH THEIR TURDS?!
SHE PICKS OUT HER VEGGIES TOO!

HEY, POOP DEVIL!!
YOUR POOP'S STUCK TO THE TOILET BOWL! I CAN'T GET IT OFF!!

WE HAD A DEAL, NO?

I'LL ALLOW YOU TO TOUCH MY CHEST...

...SO TOUCH IT!

GO ON! WHAT ARE YOU WAITING FOR? AREN'T YOU EXCITED?
TOUCH AWAY!
SHE'S AN ANGEL!
76.1

Chainsaw man

Chapter 12: Squeeze

AH ...
skweez
HWUH ?!
AHN, AHN, AHH! IT FEELS SO GOOD!
AHH ...?

PI
OP

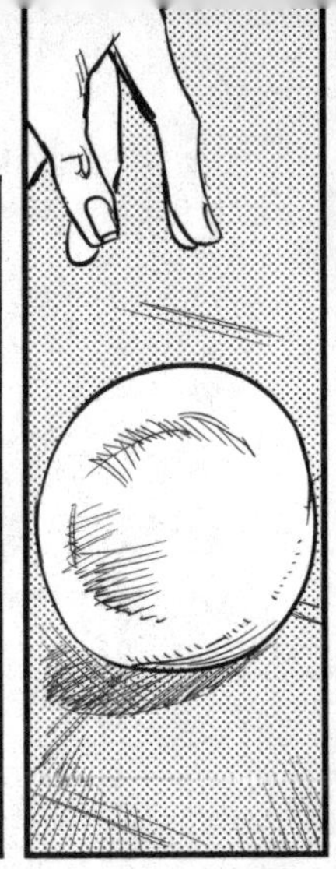

WHAT IS THIS...?

'TIS A BREAST PAD.
A WONDROUS ITEM THAT MAKES CHESTS BIGGER.

shoom
76.1

COME!
TWO SQUEEZES TO GO!
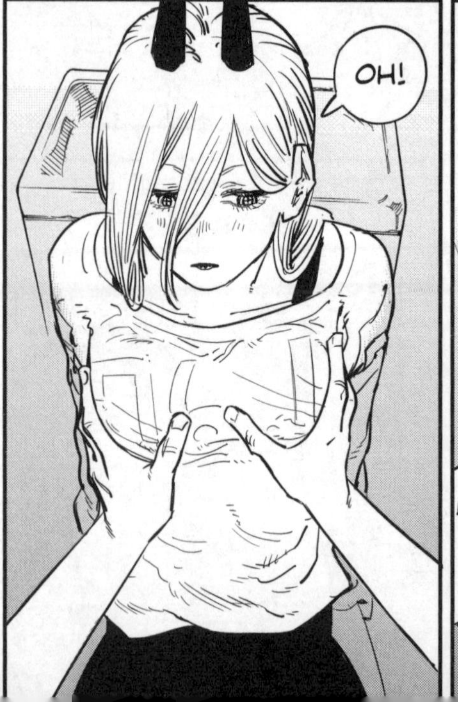
OH!

76.1

OKAY! ONE SQUEEZE LEFT!

76.1

MF.

OKAY, IT'S OVER!
TIME'S UP! WELL?! IT FELT GOOD, NO?!

SO MANY THINGS I WANNA SAY.

BUT, HUH...?

THAT'S IT...?

AREN'T YOU LUCKY, GETTING TO TOUCH SOMETHING SO NICE!

NOW WE'RE ALL SQUARE!

I LOOK FORWARD TO WORKING WITH YOU, BUDDY!

NOW THAT MEOWY'S SAFE...
...THERE'S NO REASON FOR ME TO BE A DEVIL HUNTER ANYMORE...
...BUT I CAN'T ESCAPE MAKIMA!
SO I'LL DO YOU A FAVOR AND HELP YOU WITH YOUR JOB!

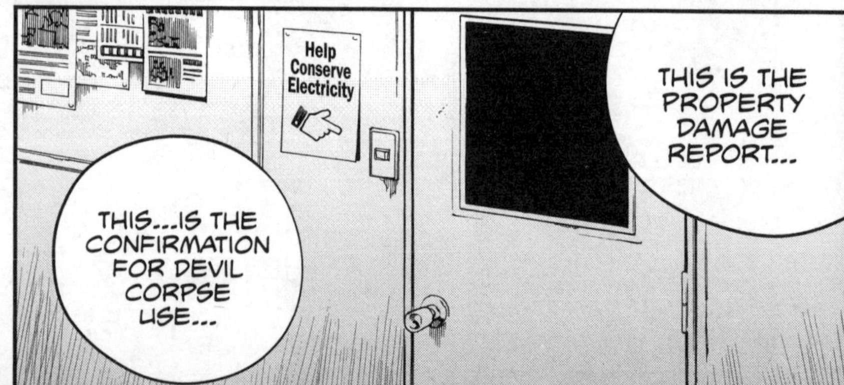
THIS IS THE PROPERTY DAMAGE REPORT...
Help Conserve Electricity
THIS...IS THE CONFIRMATION FOR DEVIL CORPSE USE...

ALSO... THIS IS FROM THE MINISTRY OF LAND, INFRA-STRUCTURE AND TRANSPORT.

FOR THIS ONE, YOU STAMP HERE AND HERE.

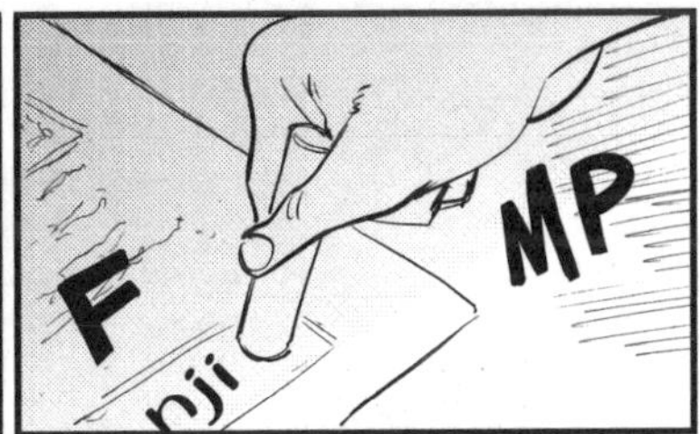

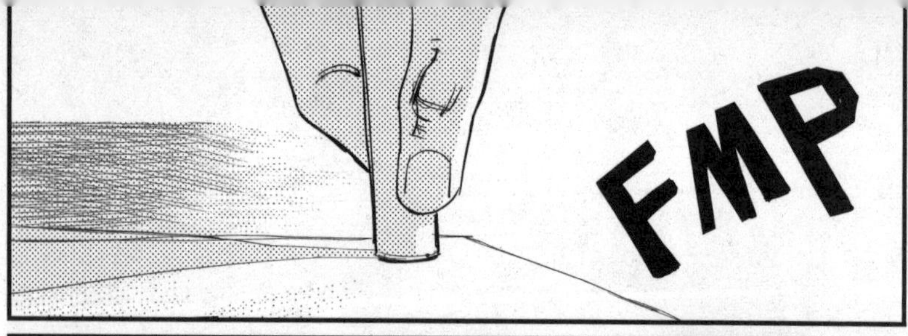
FMP

I...
I FINALLY...
...GOT AHOLD OF THIS DREAM I'D BEEN CHASING FOR THE LONGEST TIME.

BUT ONCE I ACTUALLY HAD MY HANDS ON IT...
IT WAS WAY LESS LIFE CHANGING THAN I EXPECTED...

AND NOW I'M LIKE... WHEN I GO AFTER DIFFERENT DREAMS IN THE FUTURE AND GET MY HANDS ON THEM...
...AM I GONNA REALIZE I WAS ACTUALLY HAPPIER DURING THE CHASE *THEN* TOO...?

ISN'T THAT JUST... CRAP...?

ABOUT HOW WHEN I TOUCHED BOOBS FOR THE FIRST TIME, IT TURNED OUT TO BE NO BIG DEAL...

WHAT ARE YOU TALKING ABOUT?

HMM...

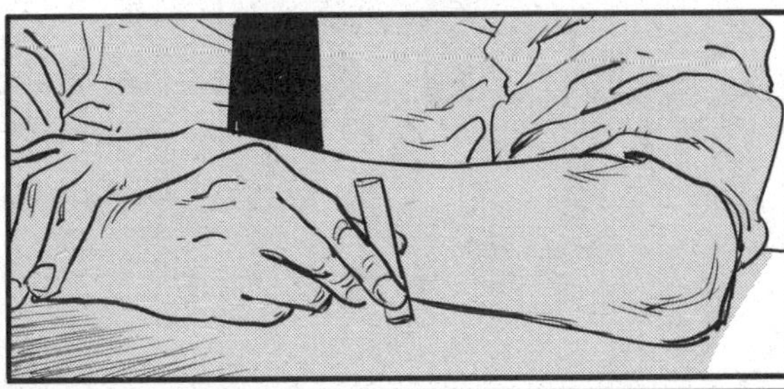

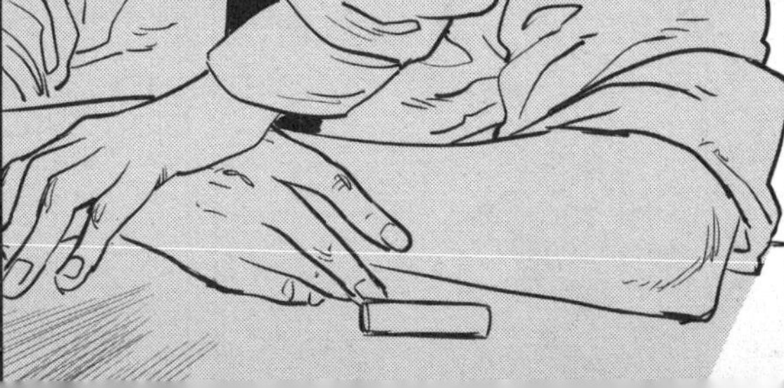

DENJI.

I THINK...

...NAUGHTY THINGS FEEL BETTER THE MORE YOU KNOW YOUR PARTNER.

IT'S DIFFICULT TO UNDERSTAND ANOTHER'S HEART...

...SO FIRST, TAKE YOUR TIME STUDYING HER HANDS...

HOW LONG ARE HER FINGERS ...?

ARE HER PALMS COLD? OR WARM?

HOW ARE HER EARS SHAPED?

HAVE YOU EVER HAD YOUR FINGER BITTEN?

BIH...
MEMO-RIZE IT.

KNOW IT SO WELL THAT EVEN IF YOU LOST YOUR SIGHT...
...YOU'D RECOG-NIZE ME BY MY BITE.

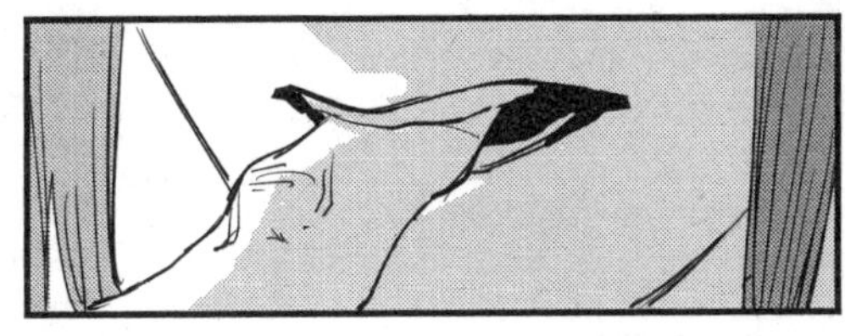

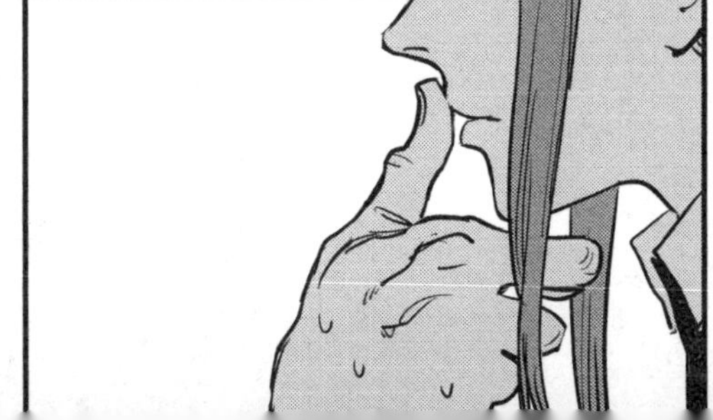

I MEMORIZED IT...

AHH?!
AH!!

KLAT
TER

AHH
...

AH...
AHH...
AHHHH...
AH...

I HAVE A FAVOR TO ASK YOU. CAN I?

OKAY.

I THINK *YOU* COULD PULL IT OFF.

BECAUSE YOU'RE MORE SPECIAL THAN ALL THE OTHER DEVIL HUNTERS.

IF YOU CAN KILL THE GUN DEVIL...

...I'LL GRANT YOU ANY ONE WISH.

Chain
saw
man

Chapter 13: Gun Devil

IT'S A DEVIL SO STRONG AND EVIL THAT IT'S OKAY TO OFFER YOU A BLANK CHECK.
Holy crap!
Is it really okay to offer me a blank check like that?!
SAY FOR INSTANCE SE—
ANYTHING, DENJI.
ANY-THING ...?

GEE... DIDN'T KNOW THERE WAS ONE THAT POWER-FUL...
THIRTEEN YEARS AGO... THERE WAS A TIME WHEN THE WHOLE WORLD TRIED TO CASH IN ON GUNS AS A COUNTER-MEASURE AGAINST THE DEVILS.
DURING THAT PERIOD, GUN USE IN CRIMES AND CIVIL REVOLTS INCREASED.

EVERY COUNTRY'S MEDIA ENDED UP COVERING GUN VIOLENCE NEWS HEAVILY...
...AND JUST WHEN FEAR OF GUNS HAD RISEN AROUND THE WORLD...
...THERE WAS A BIG TERRORIST ATTACK INVOLVING GUNS IN AMERICA.

That same day, the Gun Devil appeared.
Insect Collection
LIVE
M T W TH
1 2 3
7 8 9 10
14 15 16 17
21 22 23 24
28 29 30

The Town Mouse and the Country Mouse

"'THIS IS WHERE *I* LIVE'"...

...SAID THE TOWN MOUSE."

"WHAT A BIG HOUSE IT WAS!"

"THE TOWN MOUSE'S FAMILY..."

DAD!

COME OUTSIDE AND PLAY CATCH!

YOU'RE THE BIG BROTHER.
BE PATIENT AND PLAY BY YOURSELF.
I...
I WANNA PLAY WITH MY BIG BROTHER!
IF YOU START TO FEEL BAD, COME BACK IN THE HOUSE, OKAY?
OKAY!

splat
SKWEEN
DON'T FOLLOW ME!
YOU'RE ANNOYING!
I CAN PLAY ON MY OWN!
BOOSH

MY HANDS'RE COLD...
Huff
Huff
IF YOU CATCH A COLD, *I'LL* BE THE ONE IN TROUBLE.

YOUR HANDS WON'T GET COLD IF WE PLAY CATCH.
GO GET OUR GLOVES FROM THE HOUSE.

WOO-HOO!

KLak

November 18
10:00 a.m.
The Gun Devil hits Japan for 26 seconds.

Death toll: 57,912

United States: 124 seconds
Deaths: 548,012
China: 37 seconds
Deaths: 316,932
Canada: 7 seconds
Deaths: 8,481
Soviet Union: 210 seconds
Deaths: 155,302
Hawaii: 0.4 seconds
Deaths: 780
Mexico: 2 seconds
Deaths: 6,088
India: 15 seconds
Deaths: 29,950

AFTER THE INCIDENT, FEAR OF DEVILS AS A WHOLE SOARED, AND ALL DEVILS BECAME STRONGER THAN BEFORE.

IN AN ATTEMPT TO WEAKEN THE GUN DEVIL BY ANY AMOUNT POSSIBLE, GUN CONTROL LAWS WERE STRENGTHENED IN EVERY NATION...

...AND NEWS COVERAGE OF VIOLENT CRIME, DISASTERS AND SO ON BEGAN TO BE RESTRICTED.

Well... If I try reeally super hard...

...it should be a peace of cake!

THESE ARE PIECES OF THE GUN DEVIL'S FLESH THAT WE'VE COLLECTED.

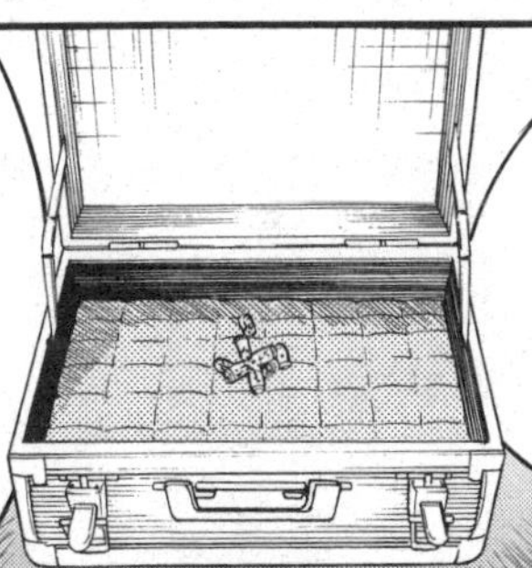
IT SEEMS LIKE THE GUN DEVIL MOVED SO FAST THAT BITS OF ITS BODY BURNED OFF.
WHEN DEVILS EAT THESE PIECES, THE GUN DEVIL'S POWER ENHANCES THEIR POWER, REGARDLESS OF WHAT TYPE OF DEVIL THEY ARE.

IF YOU PUT THE PIECES TOGETHER...

SEE? THEY ATTACH.

THE GUN DEVIL IS AN INCREDIBLY STRONG DEVIL, YOU SEE.
WHEN THE PIECES OF ITS FLESH COMBINE TO A CERTAIN SIZE, APPARENTLY THEY'LL TRY TO RETURN TO ITS BODY TO REGENERATE.
SO IF WE CAN MAKE THIS CHUNK BIGGER...

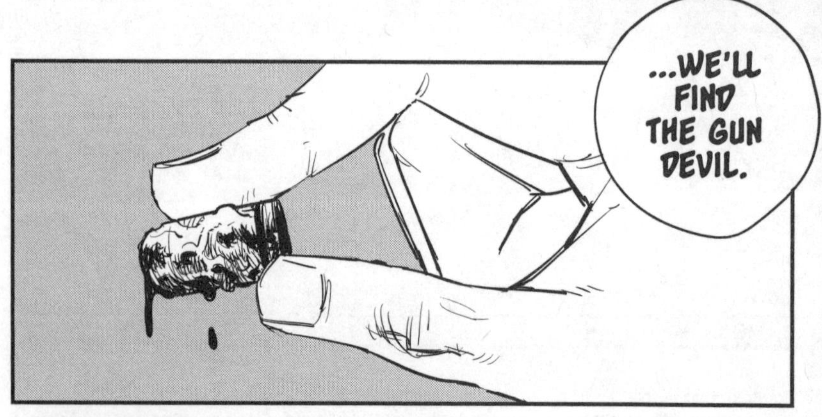

FOUND ONE.

FIGURED IT'D EATEN ONE OF THAT DAMN GUN'S CHUNKS.
IT WAS TOO STRONG FOR SOME SMALL-FRY DEVIL.

BUT DID IT EAT THAT...
...OR WAS IT FED THAT?

EITHER WAY, OUR MISSION IS THE SAME.
WE KILL ALL DEVILS.
THAT'S WHAT WILL LEAD US TO THAT THING...

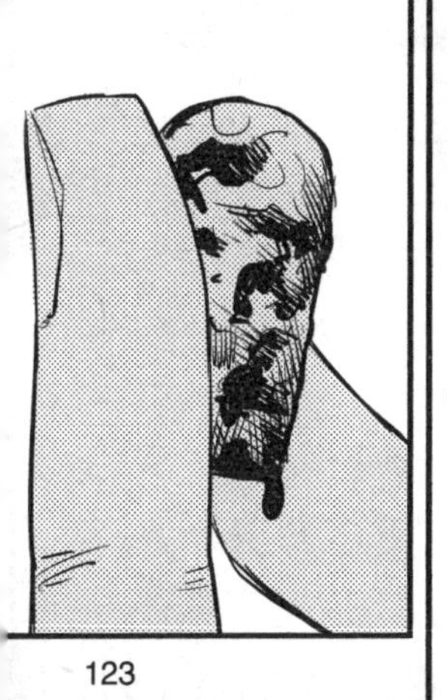

HOTEL MORIN
DEVIL EXTER-MINATION REQUEST FOR PUBLIC SAFETY.

HOTEL MORIN
DEVIL SIGHTING INSIDE MORINO HOTEL.
SURVIVAL OF HOTEL GUESTS IS UNKNOWN.
ACCORDING TO THE REQUEST, MULTIPLE CIVILIAN DEVIL HUNTERS HAVE DIED IN EXTERMINATION ATTEMPTS.

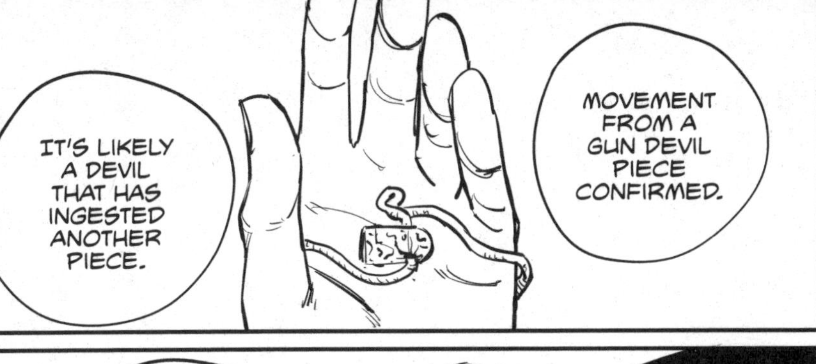
MOVEMENT FROM A GUN DEVIL PIECE CONFIRMED.
IT'S LIKELY A DEVIL THAT HAS INGESTED ANOTHER PIECE.

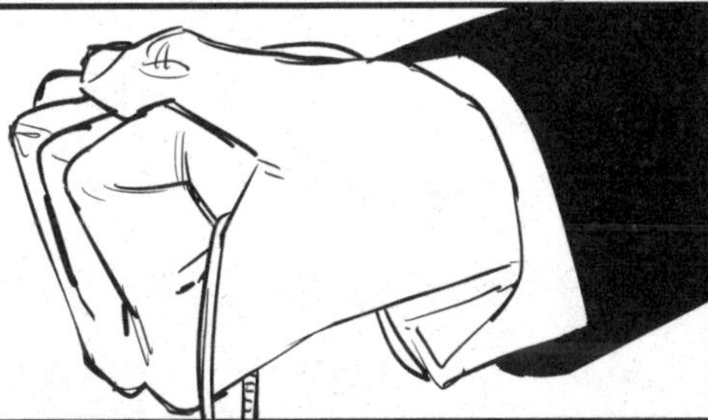
DISPATCHING SIX HUNTERS FROM PUBLIC SAFETY DEVIL EXTERMINATION SPECIAL DIVISION 4.

Chain

saw

man

Chapter 14: French Kiss

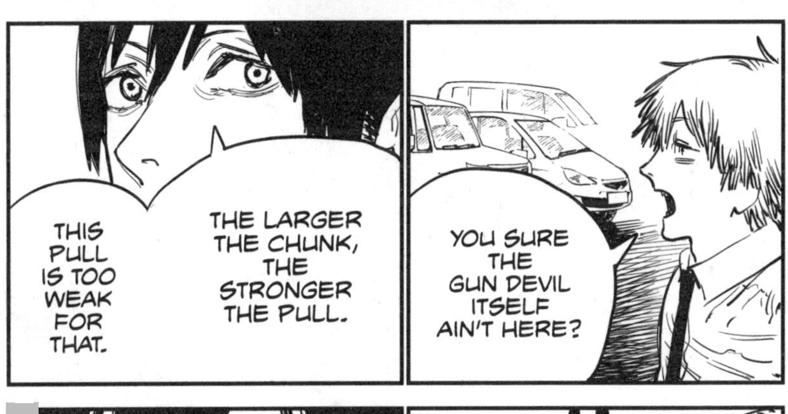

YOU TWO... DIDN'T I TELL YOU TO SPEAK RESPECT-FULLY?

HUH?

HUUH?

WHO WOULD SUCK UP TO YOU IF IT DOESN'T GET 'EM ANYTHING?!
HUMANS ARE ARROGANT FOOLS!!

GUM
GUM

HAYA-KAWA, SIR...
SIR...

BET-TER.
SWEET!
WAH!

SIR... CAN WE REALLY TRUST THOSE TWO WITH OUR BACKS?
AS TEAMMATES FIGHTING DEVILS WITH US?

ONE'S A FIEND...
AND THE OTHER IS, WELL... A STREET PUNK...
PERSONALLY, I DON'T TRUST THEM.

WE WON'T TRUST THEM WITH OUR BACKS.

WHEN WE'RE OUT ON EXTERMINATION MISSIONS, WE'LL GENERALLY HAVE THEM TAKE POINT.
IF THEY RUN AWAY, OR DOUBLE-CROSS US FOR THE DEVILS, WE'LL KILL THEM.

YOU'RE TREATING US LIKE CRAP!

YOU TWO DON'T GET HUMAN RIGHTS!

DUDE'S MEGA PISSED OFF!
MUST BE CUZ OF THAT THING THIS MORNING...

THAT PRANK DEFINITELY DID GO TOO FAR...

THAT! WAS WAY BEYOND A PRANK!!
I'LL KILL YOU!!
SCARY... WHAT THE HECK HAPPENED...?

C'MON, AKI, YOU CAN'T BE STRICT WITH THEM ALL THE TIME.

YEAH, WHAT SHE SAID! THAT BAT ALMOST KILLED ME, AND NOW IT'S STRAIGHT BACK TO WORK!
GIMME A RE-WARD!

OHO!

ALL RIGHT! I'LL THROW YOU A BONE!

duh-duuun
The Lucky winner who defeats the Devil this time geeets...
...a kiss on the cheek from me!

BWUH?!

THAT'S—THAT'S INAPPROPRIATE!
A YOUNG WOMAN SHOULDN'T GIVE HERSELF AWAY BEFORE MARRIAGE LIKE THAT!
DWUUH?!

Rii~~ght?
BUT HAVING A REWARD IS SO MUCH MORE MOTIVATING! RIGHT?!
AWWW!

EH, I'LL PASS ON THAT KISS TOO...
BUT IT'S COOL... I'M PLENTY MOTIVATED.

OH?

I ALREADY DECIDED WHO MY FIRST KISS IS GONNA BE.
LIKE, I'M GONNA COLLECT THESE MEAT CHUNKS OR WHATEVER FOR HER...
...AND THEN MURDERIZE THE GUN DEVIL. I'M NOT SMOOCHING ANYBODY TILL THEN.

YOU, KILL THE GUN DEVIL...?

WELL, NOW. PRETTY BALLSY TO SAY THAT IN FRONT OF AKI!

PLUS, I GOT TAUGHT SOMETHIN' IMPORTANT.
NAUGHTY STUFF FEELS GOOD WHEN YOU AN' YOUR PARTNER REALLY KNOW EACH OTHER.
I DON'T EVEN KNOW YOUR NAME. I COULDN'T BE LESS INTERESTED IN YOUR LIPS!

OH REEEEEALLY?

OKAY, THEN IF *YOU* TAKE DOWN THIS DEVIL...

...I'LL KISS YOU WITH *TONGUE.*

MAN, NOTHING'S MORE ENTER-TAINING THAN TEASING BOYS!
OH GOD... OHH GOD...
I WANT TO DRINK SOME BLOOD.

ACTING INDEPEN-DENTLY IS DANGER-OUS!! STOP!!
UMPH!
GAH !!
WHAM

HIMENO HAS TRAINED ME FOR HALF A YEAR. I'M IN HER DEBT!

IF SOME PUNK FROM WHO KNOWS WHERE IS GOING TO STEAL HER LIPS...

...THEN I'LL TAKE THE KISS ON THE CHEEK INSTEAD!!

MOVE IT!!

I DON'T WANT SOME GUY PRESSING UP AGAINST ME!! IT'S CREEPY!!

GO TO HELL!!

YOU AND I GOT DIFFERENT BURDENS, MAN!!

WHAT ARAI LACKS IN ACTUAL ABILITY, HE MAKES UP FOR IN DRIVE.

KOBENI'S THE OPPOSITE. TIMID, BUT PRETTY TALENTED.

HOW ABOUT YOURS?

THE BLOOD FIEND'S STRONG, BUT A HOTHEAD. IT'S STILL POSSIBLE SHE'LL BETRAY US.

AS FOR DENJI... TOO MANY UNKNOWN FACTORS. IT'S STILL TOO SOON TO SAY.

THINK THESE FOUR NEWBIES CAN *SURVIVE*?

BOTH THE NEW HUNTERS I THINK ARE STRONG...
...AND THE ONES I DON'T...
...END UP EITHER DEAD OR MOVING TO THE CIVILIAN SECTOR IN A YEAR.

YOU SURE DODGED THE QUESTION...

DON'T YOU DIE, AKI.

DON'T YOU DIE, AKI.

HIMENO... THIS IS YOUR NEW BUDDY.

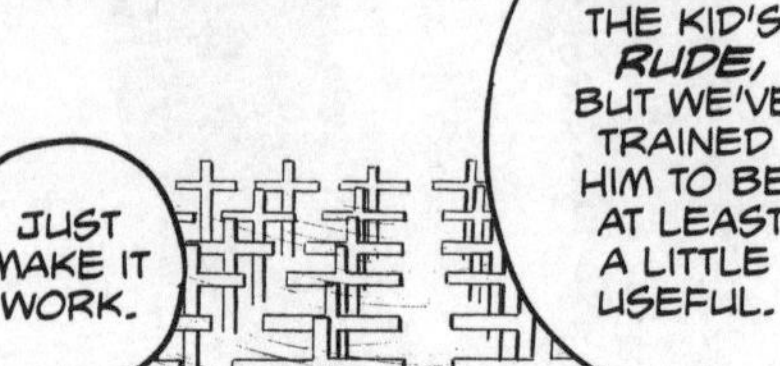
THE KID'S *RUDE,* BUT WE'VE TRAINED HIM TO BE AT LEAST A LITTLE USEFUL.
JUST MAKE IT WORK.

'SUP.
NAME'S AKI.

ARE YOU USE-FUL?

DUNNO ...
GUESS SO...

YOU'RE MY SIXTH BUDDY.

THE OTHERS ARE ALL DEAD.

THEY ALL DIED BECAUSE THEY WERE USELESS NOBODIES.

AKI...
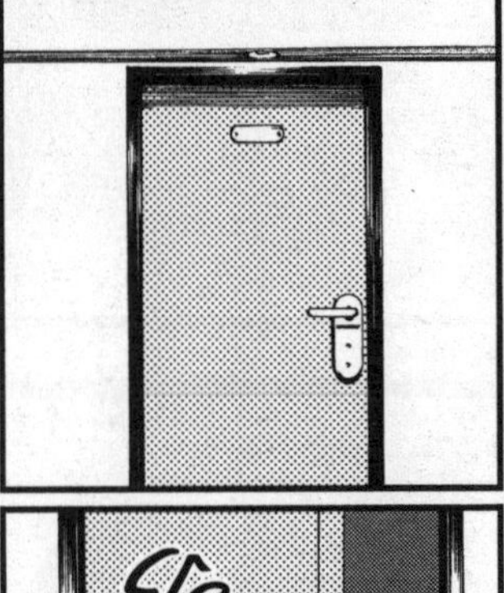

Creak

HERE IT COMES.

slap
slap
slap

Chain
saw
man

Chapter 15: Endless 8th Floor

EEP!
Eeah ...
Ah...
Ahhh !!
DWSH

CAUGHT YOU.
UH—
AWAH...
HUH?
AH...
'TIS A BATTLE!
SLISH
IT'S FLOATING...?!

SLASH

AHHH... AHH WAHH WAH...

THE DAMN DEVIL FROZE IN MIDAIR OUT OF FEAR OF ME!
GA HA HA HA HA HA!!

HOW'S IT LOOK, AKI?

ZM MM

DOES THIS THING HAVE A PIECE OF THAT DAMN GUN?

NO STRONG REAC-TION.

THIS ISN'T OUR DEVIL.

GOTCHA...

LET'S MOVE UP A FLOOR THEN!

ARE YOU SURE YOU SHOULD GO BLABBING ABOUT YOUR POWERS IN FRONT OF ME?
YOU HUMANS ARE HERE TO KEEP ME IN CHECK, NO?
IT'LL BE EASIER TO WORK AS A TEAM IF WE KNOW EACH OTHER'S POWERS, RIGHT?
PLUS, I'VE GOT A TRUMP CARD UP MY SLEEVE. IT'S ALL GOOD.

IS THAT TRUE?
THEN WHAT IF I SAID THAT I'D KILL THIS ONE? WHAT WOULD YOU DO?
nyoop
EEK!

HRK!

PUT THE WEAPON AWAY.
IF YOU MISBEHAVE, I CAN STRANGLE YOU TO DEATH ANYTIME.

OH—
GRRGH!
CAN'T TOUCH... IT...

HACK!
KEFF! KOFF!
fpp

I DON'T WANNA HAVE TO DO THAT AGAIN SO HOW ABOUT WE GET ALONG?

I'LL EAT HER ONE OF THESE DAYS!

HEY, SHE'S GONNA KISS ME. DON'T EAT HER!

WAIT, HUH ...?

WHAT IS IT?

JUST NOW... DIDN'T WE GO UP THE STAIRS FROM THE EIGHTH FLOOR TO THE NINTH?

YEAH.

FLOOR 8
THIS IS FLOOR EIGHT TOO!

YOU DIDN'T SEE WRONG OR COUNT WRONG?
NO! I'LL GO DOUBLE-CHECK!
tap
tap
tap
I'LL TURN HER INTO A STEAK AND EAT HER!

WHUH ...?
ARAI, DIDN'T YOU JUST...
...GO DOWN THE STAIRS ...?
I WANNA TRY STEAK!
HAH?
HUH? HUH? HUH?

KOBENI, MAKE DOUBLE PEACE SIGNS AND STAY COMPLETELY STILL.
HUH?

HUH? HUH? HUH? HUH?

tmp
tmp
tmp
tmp
tmp

OHHH BOY...

HUUUH?!
HUH? HUUH? HUUUH?!

AKI... WHAT THE HELL IS THIS...?

PROBABLY A DEVIL'S POWER...

KOBENI! STAY RIGHT THERE!
HUH?
WHAT THE?
WHY IS THERE A ROOM BEHIND THE WINDOW TOO...?
HUH?!
I WAS AFRAID OF THIS...

HEY! NONE OF THE WINDOWS LEAD OUTSIDE!

THEY'RE ALL CONNECTED TO THE ROOMS ON THE OPPOSITE SIDE!!

WE'RE STUCK ON THE EIGHTH FLOOR...

HERE'S THE RUNDOWN OF OUR SITUATION.
NO MATTER HOW MANY STAIRS WE CLIMB UP OR DOWN FROM THE EIGHTH-FLOOR STAIRWAY, WE ALWAYS END UP ON THE EIGHTH FLOOR. IT'S LIKELY THE HANDIWORK OF A DEVIL.

WE CAN'T USE THE ELEVATORS FOR SOME REASON.

WE CAN'T GET OUTSIDE THROUGH THE ROOMS OR WINDOWS.

WE TRIED CLIMBING UP THROUGH THE CEILING, BUT THE EIGHTH FLOOR WAS ABOVE THAT TOO.

ISN'T IT CUZ POWER WENT AND KILLED THAT DEVIL?
I BET THAT DEVIL USED ITS POWER TO TRAP US IN HERE, AND THEN IT DIED WITHOUT TURNING IT OFF!

YOU SAID TO KILL IT!
Did NOT!

DEVILS' POWERS ARE UNDONE WHEN THEY DIE. SO THAT'S IMPOSSIBLE.

AKI, ANY MOVEMENT FROM THE FLESH PIECE?
ABOUT THAT... IT COM-PLETELY STOPPED MOVING.

SO WE WALKED STRAIGHT INTO A TRAP, WITH THAT DEVIL AS THE BAIT...
THIS IS THE FIRST TIME I'VE HAD A DEVIL TRY ANYTHING THIS TRICKY.

BUT... WHEN WE DON'T COME BACK...
...WON'T OTHER DEVIL HUNTERS COME TO RESCUE US...?
WE CAN ONLY PRAY THAT THEY WON'T GET TRAPPED LIKE US.

WE'RE ALL GOING TO DIE HERE...
WE'RE GOING TO STARVE TO DEATH...

K-KOBENI! STAY STRONG!
YOU'RE WORKING AS A DEVIL HUNTER BECAUSE YOU WANT TO PUT YOUR OLDER BROTHER THROUGH COLLEGE, REMEMBER?!

I WAS HALF FORCED INTO IT...
MY PARENTS ONLY CARE ABOUT MY GIFTED BROTHER... THEY WANT TO PUT HIM THROUGH COLLEGE, SO THEY PUT *ME* TO WORK...
MY ONLY OPTIONS WERE TO BE A SEX WORKER OR A DEVIL HUNTER!

I WANTED TO GO TO COLLEGE TOO!!
BUT I'M GONNA DIE HERE!!

GA HA!
GA HA HA HA HA HA HA HA!!
THAT FACE!
GA HA HA HA HA HA HA HA!!

WHY, YOU ...!
DON'T LAUGH!!

OH, KOBENI... FEAR IS A DEVIL'S FAVORITE FOOD.
IF YOU ACT SCARED, YOU'LL BE GIVING THEM EXACTLY WHAT THEY WANT.
BUT I'M SO SCARED!!

IT'S POSSIBLE THAT TIME IS STOPPED ONLY ON THE EIGHTH FLOOR BY A DEVIL POWER.

IN WHICH CASE HELP MAY NEVER COME.

THAT'S AMAZING! THEN WE CAN SLEEP AS MUCH AS WE WANT!!

ARE YOU STUPID ...?
WE COULD BE TRAPPED HERE *FOREVER...*

IT MIGHT TURN OUT THAT WAY, AND IT MIGHT NOT, RIGHT?
WAKE ME UP WHEN YOU FIGURE IT OUT.

THESE BEDS ARE SO COMFY.

IT'D BE A WASTE NOT TO SLEEP IN 'EM.

I'MMA APPRECIATE THIS DEVIL AN' CATCH ME SOME Z'S...

HE FELL ASLEEP ...

Chain saw man

Chapter 16: First Taste

AKI'S BEEN HUNTING FOR THE DEVIL NONSTOP.
I'VE BEEN TRYING TO GET HIM TO TAKE A BREAK, BUT HE WON'T LISTEN.

ARAI WAS HELPING AKI AT FIRST...

...BUT NOW HE'S FREAKING OUT. HE SHUT HIMSELF UP IN A ROOM AND WON'T COME OUT.

KOBENI LOST IT AND TRIED TO DRINK FROM A TOILET.
SO I KNOCKED HER OUT.

AND THEN THERE'S THE FIEND...

POWER? WHAT ABOUT HER?

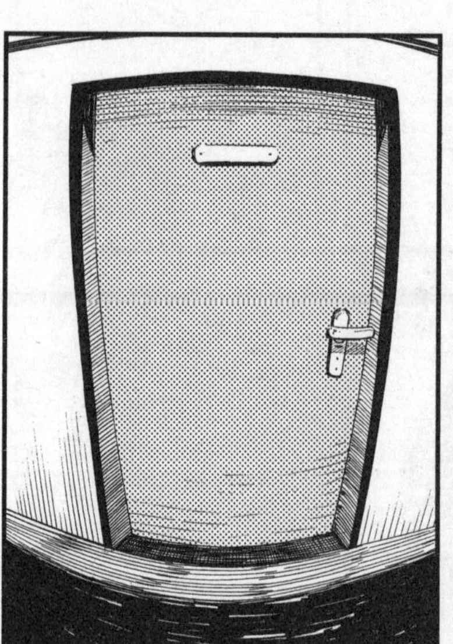

I'M BORED, SO I WAS THINKING UP A NOBEL PRIZE-WINNING INVENTION!

IF I WIN A NOBEL PRIZE, HUMANS WILL GROVEL BEFORE ME!

AND THEN I'LL USE MY NOBEL PRIZE AS A STEPPING-STONE TO BECOME PRIME MINISTER!

I WANT TO WATCH HUMANS SUFFER...

...SO MY FIRST ACT AS PRIME MINISTER WILL BE TO IMPLEMENT A 100 PERCENT SALES TAX!

SHE SEEMS THE SAME AS ALWAYS TO ME.

OH. THAT'S... GOOD THEN.

THE THREE OF US WILL GUARD KOBENI AND ARAI.
CAN'T EVEN TAKE A BATHROOM BREAK IF I'M THE ONLY ONE DOING IT.
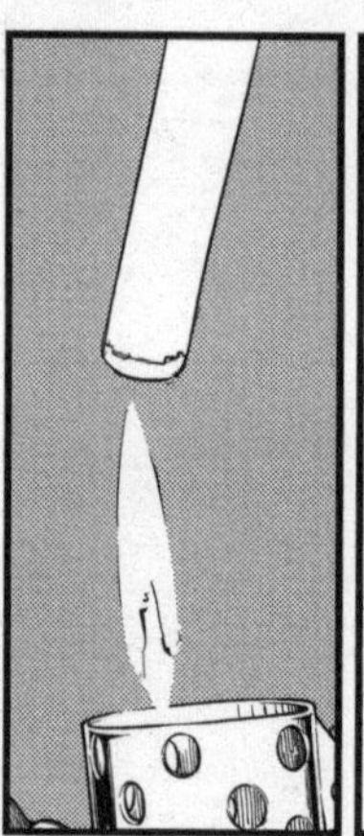

DARN. DOWN TO MY LAST CIGA-RETTE!

YOU TWO ARE TOO CALM. IT'S NO FUN!

SINCE AKI'S ON THE JOB RIGHT NOW, I CAN TAKE IT EASY AND RELAX.

PLUS, IT'S THE POWER OF NICOTINE.

IT'S SO GREAT HAVING AN ADDICTION.
IN THIS LIFE, YOU NEED SOMETHING TO TAKE THE EDGE OFF.
HEY, THAT'S THE SAME BRAND THAT JERK SMOKES.

THAT'S BECAUSE I'M THE ONE WHO TAUGHT AKI TO APPRECIATE THE TASTE OF CIGARETTES.

AKI, YOU DON'T SMOKE?

NO. IT'LL ROT YOUR BONES.

WE'RE GONNA BE WORKING TOGETHER CLOSELY, SO YOU SHOULD DO IT TOO.

I'M NOT HERE TO MAKE FRIENDS.

LET ME GUESS. YOU CAME TO PUBLIC SAFETY...
...TO KILL THE GUN DEVIL, RIGHT?

SINCE WE'RE THE ONLY ONES ALLOWED TO CARRY PIECES OF THAT DAMN GUN.
IT'S THE SAME FOR ALL THE DARK AND BROODING TYPES WHO JOIN PUBLIC SAFETY.
US DEVIL HUNTERS DON'T LIVE LONG ANYWAY. IT'S NOT LIKE THE SMOKING'S GONNA KILL YOU.
I WON'T BITE IT SO EASILY.
YOU'D BETTER NOT.
IT'S A HASSLE WHEN MY BUDDIES DIE ON ME...

AH...

HUH?

AKI. MAKE YOURSELF SCARCE, WILL YOU?
KUBOCHAN
本
あいる

ハイテク
テレビ
アジサイ

slap

WHAT WAS THAT ABOUT?

SHE WAS MY PREVIOUS BUDDY'S GIRLFRIEND.

IT'S PRETTY COMMON FOR THERE TO BE TROUBLE WITH YOUR LATE BUDDIES' FAMILIES AND SO ON.

WHAT DID YOU JUST DO...?

I SNUCK UP TO HER AND STUCK GUM ON HER.

WHUH?

AN EYE FOR AN EYE, A TOOTH FOR A TOOTH.

IT'S NOT YOUR PROBLEM— IT PISSED *ME* OFF.

SO I RETALIATED.

SERVES HER RIGHT. NOW SHE HAS GUM ON HER CLOTHES, AND SHE HAS NO IDEA.

HA...

AH HA HA HA HA HA HA HA!!

3F
中華点々
2F
Tenten Chinese Restaurant
YOU REMINDED ME OF SOMETHING MY MASTER ALWAYS SAID.
"THE DEVIL HUNTERS THAT THE DEVILS FEAR MOST AREN'T THE STRONG OR THE BRAVE..."
"...THEY'RE AFRAID OF THE ONES WITH A FEW SCREWS LOOSE."
I THINK YOU'LL MANAGE TO LIVE FOR A LONG WHILE.
IS THAT SOME KIND OF INSULT?
IF YOU'RE NOT GONNA EAT THAT ALMOND TOFU, I'M TAKING IT.

I'LL GIVE YOU A CIGARETTE.
I DON'T SMOKE. IT'LL ROT YOUR BONES.
THIS SEEMS LIKE IT'LL BE A LONG RELATIONSHIP, SO I SURE WOULD LIKE IT IF YOU SMOKED...
FINE, I'LL SMOKE IT. BUT JUST THE ONE.
THIS IS THE ONLY CIGARETTE I'LL SMOKE IN MY ENTIRE LIFE.

HIMENO... DO YOU HAVE ANY CIGARETTES LEFT?

SORRY! THIS IS MY LAST ONE!

THEN LET ME HAVE THAT ONE.
SERIOUSLY? YOU HOPELESS ADDICT.

HOOO

SHUT UP.

That's a kiss!
An indirect kiss! No fair!!

I'VE GOT BAD NEWS.

REMEMBER THAT DEVIL WE KILLED...?

YOU MEAN THE ONE I KILLED!

YEAH, WELL, IT'S GOTTEN BIGGER... A LOT BIGGER...

I THOUGHT I KILLED IT...

TRAPPING US IN THIS HOTEL...
A FORM LIKE NOTHING I'VE SEEN BEFORE...
WHAT KIND OF DEVIL IS THIS THING?

HUMAN.
HUMANS.
FOOLISH HUMANS.
I'LL OFFER YOU A CONTRACT.

IT SPOKE!
A CONTRACT ...?

LET ME EAT THAT HUMAN NAMED DENJI...
DEAD OR ALIVE...
FEED HIM TO ME...
...AND I'LL RETURN ALL OF YOU OTHER DEVIL HUNTERS TO THE OUTSIDE UNHARMED.
I'LL RETURN YOU UN-HARMED...
MAKE A CONTRACT WITH ME...

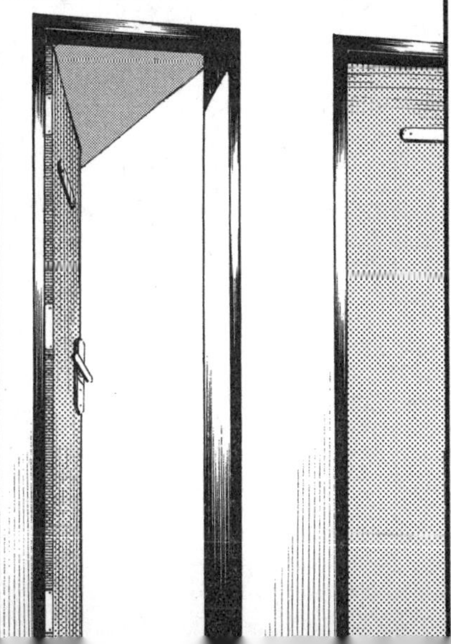

TO BE CONTINUED...

Chain saw man

Denji & Pochita's Staple Dish

Chain saw man

THIS PLACE HAS GOOD COFFEE.

OH YEAH? I'VE NEVER HAD COFFEE BEFORE.
gulp

GROSS! THIS STUFF IS MUDDY WATER!

WHAT A FOOL! A KID WOULDN'T APPRECIATE THE TASTE OF COFFEE!
SLURP

BLEURGH
HRLP...!
DITCH-WATER!!

SHUT UP! BE QUIET INSIDE THE RESTAU-RANT!
Hey! You tricked us! This is mud!
'TIS DITCHWATER YOU DRINK!!

YOU'RE READING THE WRONG WAY!

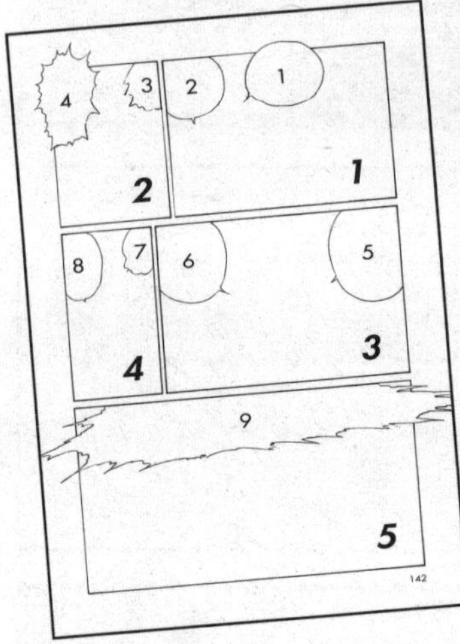

Chainsaw Man reads from right to left, starting in the upper-right corner. Japanese is read from right to left, meaning that action, sound effects and word-balloon order are completely reversed from English order.